M000033914

SECRET POSTINGS

Bletchley Park to The Pentagon

Charlotte Webb

First Published by BookTower Publishing 2011
Redditch, Worcestershire
www.booktowerpublishing.co.uk

Second Edition Published 2014
© Charlotte Webb

Charlotte Webb asserts the moral right to to be identified as the editor of
this work.

A catalogue record for this book is available from the
British Library

Book Cover & Interior Design Kerry Howard
www.bletchleyparkresearch.co.uk

BookTower Publishing
ISBN 978-0-9557164-7-8

BookTower
PUBLISHING

For my parents
Without their love, help and encouragement my life would
have been the poorer.

CONTENTS

ACKNOWLEDGMENTS

Without a great deal of encouragement and help this insight into the past would not have been possible. Therefore my grateful thanks go to members of my family, Judith Frames and Kerry Howard.

FOREWORD

Although this is mainly a personal record spanning the major part of a century, readers may find it interesting to compare the relatively simple way in which we lived before the advent of the many forms of 'must have' equipment, such as washing machines, dishwashers, telephones, computers etc, which most of us take for granted today. Looking back over the last eighty plus years, I realise how fortunate I am to have lived through such interesting and progressive times.

"There is nowhere else quite like Bletchley Park.
There is no comparison to make."
Sir John Scarlett
KCMG, OBE

CHAPTER ONE

CIVILIAN TO SERVICE

Thinking back I can see myself as an eighteen year old listening to the news on the wireless, wishing I could do more for the war effort. That May afternoon was the start of a journey that would take me to the Government Code and Cypher School's covert operation at Bletchley Park and then, after the European war had ended in May 1945, on to The Pentagon in Washington D.C. to see out the remainder of the war against Japan.

It was May 1941 and the bombing of Britain, known as the Blitz, had ended. I was halfway through a Domestic Science Course at Radbrook College near Shrewsbury to learn how cook, run a house and do household accounts.

Radbrook students were allowed to go into Shrewsbury on Saturdays but had to be back in college by 9.30pm. I laugh when I remember the number of films we never got to see the end of.

It was hard to focus on our studies when the Blitz had seen the destruction or damage to over one million homes since September 1940. Due to food shortages, it was also difficult to remain enthusiastic about cooking colourless food from simplified war time recipes.

During the two terms I had been at Radbrook there was a growing restlessness and for some of us our daily lives became increasingly frustrating. For me, illness exacerbated my dissatisfaction during which a bout of measles and chickenpox meant a period of isolation with only 'Gone With The Wind' by Margaret Mitchell as refuge against the boredom.

Charlotte Vine-Stevens 1939 © Charlotte Webb

It was listening to the bad news of the war on the wireless that day in May that fuelled my dissatisfaction and inspired me to leave the course and join up. Four of us chose to leave – surely we could contribute more to the War effort?

At that time, joining the Women's Services was voluntary as conscription of women had not started and I had to choose between the Auxiliary Territorial Service (ATS), Women's Royal Naval Service (WRNS) or the Women's Auxiliary Air Force (WAAF) without understanding the function each service provided. I made my choice based on the qualifications I had gained through home schooling and, like many other women, the attractiveness of the service uniform! Based on those criteria, my first choice was the popular WRNS but there were no vacancies, so I applied and was accepted for the ATS.

Established by Royal Warrant on 9 September 1938 the ATS was part of the British Army and was initially attached to the Territorial Army. By the time I joined on 3 September 1941, the ATS had been granted full military status and there were sixty five thousand of us serving our country. The military status ensured that officers received a commission and rank in the same way as the male officers, but unfortunately we did not get equal pay. As more men joined the war, more women volunteered but the continued pressure to support the war effort prompted the coming into force of the National Service Act in December 1941, which called up all unmarried women between the ages of twenty and thirty years old to join one of the women's services. Women who were not conscripted for one reason or another were required to help the war effort by taking jobs previously held by men or new jobs, such as in munitions factories.

By September 1943 the number of women serving in the ATS peaked at 212,500 before the numbers began to decline gradually until the end of the war. The ATS was disbanded in 1949 and replaced on 1 February 1949 by the Women's Royal Army Corps (WRAC).

CHAPTER TWO

LIFE IN THE COUNTRYSIDE

Life in the ATS came as a big culture shock for me. Growing up in Richard's Castle, a village four and a half miles from Ludlow in the scenic Herefordshire Countryside was a million miles away from living in close quarters with hundreds of other girls, where space and privacy were rare.

My clearest childhood memory dates back to September 1927 about the time I was four years of age and my brother David died. I had been staying in the village with the Hall family, who often 'gave a hand' as David had struggled with ill health since his birth on 31 January 1925. On walking back up the front path to the family home, 'Ryecroft', I asked 'where is David?' and was told to 'ssh'. I think I sensed that he had died but I cannot remember how I coped after then.

'Ryecroft' is the name of the three acres of grassland raised above Woodhouse Lane that made up our family home. From the bungalow we looked out onto an extensive view from Clee Hill (Titterstone) in the east along to Abberley, and Stoke

Edith. The property was, and still is, surrounded by many trees – Copper Beech, Spanish and Horse Chestnut, Norwegian Spruce, Yew and many varieties of fruits and shrubs. We lived on our own fruit and vegetable crops, a small apiary, goats, pigs and poultry.

Charlotte Vine-Stevens at home in Ryecroft 1925/26
© Charlotte Webb

There was no gas, electricity nor mains water, so heating was by open coal or wood fires and water was pumped from a well under the bungalow. Cooking was by Valor paraffin stoves and lighting by paraffin lamps and candles.

Sometimes we gave luncheon parties, when mother would boast that everything on the table was home produced. On one occasion when chicken was served I asked whether it was 'Hilda?' Poor mother, what an awful thing to say – no doubt I was put in my place, but I don't recall it.

The latrines at Ryecroft were quite a walk from the house, which was not funny when it was pouring with rain or one needed to go in a hurry! The journey took you from the back door, along the hedge adjacent to the house, past the back of the bee hives to the honeysuckle covered privy. The building was covered by an enormous yew tree, hiding its existence to those not knowing where to look.

Groceries were delivered from Ludlow every two weeks. Messrs. Stephens travelled round collecting the orders one week and delivering the next. A 'bus (Holt's) ran in and out of Ludlow, stopping at every house if needed, twice on Saturdays and once on Mondays. It was used mainly by cottagers and small-holders taking their produce to Ludlow market.

The bus was always crammed full of men and women chattering away in the local dialect (broad Herefordshire) and when the bus slithered to halt in the narrow lanes to pick up more passengers who appeared from the cottages without warning, there would be cries of 'Oh my God, my eggs!' as the owners clung onto their baskets.

My Father, who was employed by Lloyds Bank, commuted to Ludlow by motor cycle and in deep snow he walked! We did not get a family car until 1938 so when we needed to travel by train we were taken by pony and trap, driven by Jack Pugh, a local farmer to Woofferton Station, a busy junction on the Great Western Railway (GWR) lines to Birmingham and the North South line between Crewe and Bristol. I can still remember the intense cold and feel the stinging chilblains which enveloped us on the pony and trap trips.

What we lacked in 'mod cons' was more than compensated for in the lush countryside, the fresh air and freedom of the open space. I remember that I slept in a tent in the garden most of the summer free from worries about thieves, traffic and noise. On fine nights I took my bed out so that I could lie and gaze at the stars and try to comprehend the infinite distances. By November my mother urged me to sleep indoors, which with reluctance I did.

Our problems tended to be weather related. There seemed to be more snow in those days and it lodged in the corrugated iron roof gables and seeped through into the bedrooms. Then, often, there were droughts in the summers when the well dried up and so did the waterbutts. A bowl of clean water was used to wash the vegetables, then the dishes and finally on to plants in the garden. Daily bathing was out of the question during long droughts.

My sister, Margaret, arrived in the night of 29 September 1930 in the bedroom next to mine. The following year Mother had a mastectomy and subsequently had to have radium treatment in Birmingham. She was one of the first women to survive the operation. We were fortunate; there were always lads and lassies available to do jobs in the house and garden. There was much poverty and people were glad of a meal as payment for work. We also had an au pair from Germany (Tänte Moderau) in the early thirties and later Clara Mandli (now Buchmann) from Zurich. She rang me on 13 May 2008 from an old people's home – I believe she was ninety six at the time. Because my mother, Clara Mandli and Tänte Moderau conversed in German we soon became bi-lingual with a pretty good accent.

Mother must have had an iron will for she carried on with so much for 30 years before she died: coping with the animals, teaching us and doing endless charitable things in the village including setting up basket making classes using the osiers, a species of willow, we grew to teach unemployed men in the village to make a living out of basket-making.

She was an organist, pianist and singer and played classical pieces to help us go to sleep every evening. She taught us to play the piano. We also had violin lessons. I found the violin very difficult and could have been a better pianist if I had worked harder at it – but if nothing else I learned to appreciate good music and it is still part of my life. Mother sang in a choir conducted by Sir Edward Elgar.

We were educated under the Parents National Educational Union (PNEU) System which covered a broad spectrum of subjects. We also had private tuition with Miss Faraday (a niece of Michael Faraday, the scientist). I was hopeless at exams and never achieved any good results, apart from being able to speak fairly good German and I taught myself Spanish which has been quite useful with translating the Spanish edition of the Organisation of American States Magazine, shopping in Spain and Tenerife as well as trying to understand my hairdresser in Chile – I must say that was the most difficult! To me the Chilean Spanish has quite a dialect, but I enjoyed practicing many years later during a month's stay in Chile with relatives.

In 1935 (I was 12 years old) my parents and I attended a gathering of PNEU members at the headquarters in Ambleside, in the Lake District. In Pageant I took the part of Lady Elizabeth Woodville. There I met Pleione and Martha Kingdon-Ward with whom I kept in touch for several years. Little did I know that their father would become a well-known botanist. I discovered this while on holiday in Canada in 1999 where I found his name in a memorial garden.

In his spare time, Dad worked hard in the garden and we had all the fruit and vegetables one could possibly want. His main hobby was cricket and he played for the Ludlow and South Shropshire team for whom Mother would often provide afternoon tea for the players with homemade bread and cakes. The cricket ground was about 8 miles from home – far enough on a bicycle with the provisions in the basket! I did NOT like having to sit 'quietly' whilst the match was being played.

Many of the farms and cottages were part of the Moor Park Estate, nestled in the countryside between Richard's Castle and Ludlow, or belonged to the former Lord of the Manor, Mr Roger Salwey, whose family goes back many hundred years: I recall one of their gravestones in the old village churchyard, St Bartholomew's, dated 1500. Lancing College was evacuated to Moor Park during World War II, following which it was sold off and has continued to be used as a school.

In the new village church, All Saints, we had our allocated seats – the Salweys in the front row of the left hand aisle, behind them Captain Ronnie Wallace and the Kennedy family from the Lodge, and the Windsor-Clives (Clive of India). We sat behind them. On the right hand side the Betton-Fosters and the Alcock family had pride of place and the rest of the community sat behind them.

Charlotte Vine-Stevens, 1937 © Charlotte Webb

The organ needed water to activate the bellows and the supply came from Boney Well which was not always consistent because some of the houses between the well and the church were also supplied from the same pipeline. Mrs Alcock played for the services: Leipzig Conservatoire trained, she was excellent. Mother played the organ from time to time, putting her music talent to good use.

In the church there is a Roll of Honour for those from the village who served in the World War II. Only John Haggart died in action. He did not return from Arnhem. I am proud to say the Roll of Honour includes my name.

CHAPTER THREE

TIME OF WAR

Dad joined the Royal West Kent Regiment as an Army Officer direct from school (Rochester King's School) in 1914. He served in Mesopotamia (re-named Iraq) and India, returning to the UK in 1918.

Sometime between 1918 and my parent's wedding in 1920 he began working for Lloyds Bank in Ludlow. They lived in 'The Villa' in Aston on Clun, where I was born.

An active member of the local branch of the British Legion, he was selected to serve in 1938 in the British Legion Police Force in Czechoslovakia. The mission was aborted within weeks – Dad's report on this, in full, can be found at the back of this book.

Mother had been a music teacher in a school in Germany for a year from August 1914 until August 1915. World War I broke out on the 4 August 1914, the day Mother travelled to Germany and arrived at the school near Leipzig. No attempt to stop her was made at customs, nor was she turned back upon arrival. However, she was classed as the enemy and obliged to report to the local police station each day, although as time went by the police became quite friendly and simply acknowledged her with a wave each day. After a year's negotiations with the American Embassy in Berlin she was granted safe passage to return to the UK. Unfortunately, we never had the opportunity to talk more about her time there.

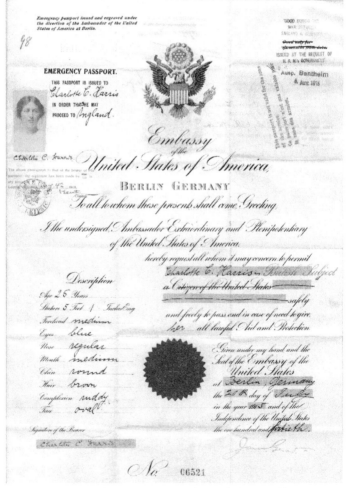

Passport from Germany, 1914   © Charlotte Webb

My first experience of Germany came in 1937 through an exchange visit with Elisabeth Paul (pronounced Powell), who came from a little town called Herrnhut in Saxony, near Dresden. She came to us for three months through the summer to improve her English and for me to improve my German by staying with her family in Germany. Elizabeth and I were of a similar age but from very different backgrounds.

The journey started from Ludlow on a train to London where my great uncle Cecil Stockton met us and gave us a whistle stop tour of London to fill the hours until our next train to Harwich. As a London resident Uncle Cecil showed us the sites with which he was very familiar. I had a lot of luggage because (at that time) it was customary for washing to be done every six weeks so it was necessary to take six of every item of underwear.

From Harwich we boarded a ferry to Flushing (Holland). The final leg of the overnight train journey to Dresden was very tiring and very uncomfortable. I couldn't sleep and felt rather miserable. After four days on the way it was a relief to arrive in Dresden where Elizabeth's mother met us and showed us something of the city. We went to an historical jousting tournament before going on to the Paul family home in Herrnhut.

I felt very homesick and miserable throughout the journey, which was about a thousand miles. Elisabeth's family and Tante Moderau met us and we moved on to the Paul family home in Herrnhut where I lived and went to school. I soon settled down and began to enjoy my visit. My German was reasonable but not good enough to do essays or exams.

Herrnhut had a very strong Moravian (Brudergemeine)

community – very religious. Traditionally men and women sat separately on opposite sides of church during church services and the women wore significant bonnets. Widows wore black bonnets, married women wore blue and singles, pink. The 'Bonnets' were made of a pretty netting and tied under the chin with ribbons.

Sometimes the choir was accompanied by four string instruments and listening to the violin I was inspired to play myself. Eventually I did, and with my sister Margaret, became part of "The Little Orchestra' in Ludlow, which was conducted by Gerhard Haase, who had been taken prisoner and placed in a Prisoner of War (POW) camp in Ludlow (a house called The Sheet). He and other German POWs were all artists of one sort or another and had no interest in being in the German Army. Gerhard married one of the orchestra members (Nan Chesters), became nationalised and stayed in this country.

It was a very quiet, understated community and their clothing rather similar to English styles, except the bonnets. I do remember that they had a sort of duvet, similar to what is commonly used today. At home, at that time we were still using sheets and blankets. It was common in German houses to have a solid fuel Ofen – an enclosed stove in the centre of the room. The family lived high up in a block of flats with a balcony overlooking the green surrounding landscape. There also seemed to be a shortage of butter. I know not why!

During my stay I was included in many of their social activities including family weddings and christenings. I also attended school, which started at 7am and ended at 1.30pm. The afternoons were always filled with sports. One particular day stands out in my mind when the school went to a farm on the Czech border to harvest potatoes – I was stiff the next day.

(From left) Elisabeth & Erdmuth Paul, Charlotte Vine-Stevens, 1937
© Charlotte Webb

In school we were obliged to stand to attention and give the Hitler salute at the beginning and end of every class. Herrnhut was the main Brudergemeine (Moravian church), which exists in several other countries including Great Britain. I did not fully comprehend the German threat but felt it was diplomatic to join in with the class requirement to salute. I disguised my discomfort by waving my arms but not joining the verbal salute. I certainly felt an undercurrent of concern.

Herr Paul did try to convey to me the local anxiety about the political situation and Hitler regime but my German was not good enough to fully understand his words. Elisabeth and Erdmuth aged fourteen and twelve were obliged to belong to the Bund Deutches Madels (as far as I could make out it was a very military set up). They disappeared every Sunday morning but I was not allowed to attend as a guest. I was aware that it was a requirement but Herr Paul and his wife were not happy that their children joined in. It was never discussed by the parents and Elisabeth never talked to me of it.

I remember an anxious time when Erdmuth had scarlet fever and even though were all shared wooden bunks in the same room I was lucky enough not to catch it. On October 20th she went into Zittau Hospital on the Czech border. Although she was very ill she made a full recovery.

Living with the family and meeting their friends and relations was a good experience but I was glad to be home again. I kept in touch with the Paul family in Herrnhut until World War II broke out and did not hear from them again, which I regret.

I still have a postcard my host sent to my parents and brings back many fond memories of my time with his family:

Dear Mr. Vine-Stevens,

Herewith I thank you for the friendly sent views of Betty. Furthermore I confirm to you the receipt of the 50 Deutschmark which I received in two traveller cheques from your bank, which I handed over to your daughter Betty. Betty is very happy with my 2 girls, especially Elisabeth, we see them often happy together. We, my wife and I, have become quite fond of Betty, as she integrates with our family and also helps my wife in the household. In school it seems that she understands almost everything well, her German speaking becomes better every day! We often play music together, which we all love a lot! We already look for a companion for the return journey for Betty. I myself have a lot of work to do with the creation of my business premises.

With best regards to you and your wife.

I am very sincerely

Gerhard Paul

In the summer of 1938, we went on a rare family holiday to Fairbourne on the Welsh coast. There I met my first 'boyfriend', Otto Stoetzer. I was fifteen and he seventeen. He was on holiday from Germany. Fluent in German, Spanish and French, I thought he was the 'bees knees' and was delighted to be able to air my German. We corresponded until war broke out and met again after the war but a lasting romance was not to be. However, he sent me the Spanish version of the Organisation of American States Magazine regularly from Buenos Aires so I was able to keep up limited Spanish and learn a lot about South America and its problems.

Also, in 1938 Dorothea Schiffer joined us from Breslau in Germany: her father was Jewish and a Doctor of Medicine. Her mother came from an aristocratic family (the von Braunschweigs) who died before Dorothea came away from the gathering Nazi regime. She soon became one of the family and stayed until training as a children's nurse in London. We remained good friends until she died in 1966 of cancer. I felt very lost without her and still do, but her daughter, Hella, whom I consider an adopted niece, is a delight and we are in close touch even though she and her family live on Barra in the Outer Hebrides.

As soon as War was declared on 3 September 1939, Dad became an officer in the Home Guard. He had a large area to oversee on the Herefordshire, Shropshire and Worcestershire borders. At least he had some petrol, but of course we could not use it unless we happened to be going where he was on duty!

To begin with the LDV (later Home Guard), were not issued with weapons but when they did arrive, Dad had to store them in our house until they were issued to his men. There was nowhere to put them out of sight except under my parent's four poster bed. We were all very relieved to see the back of them.

CHAPTER FOUR

TRAINING FOR WAR

The war changed many lives, and mine was no exception. It affected us in the country probably much less than those in our towns and cities. There was more to eat and while we often heard enemy planes passing overhead we were spared the horrors of bombing raids that devastated other towns and cities. We did see the flashes of light beyond Clee Hill as bombs fell on Birmingham over fifty miles away. Between April 1940 and August 1943 Birmingham became the third heaviest bombed city in the country.

My calling up papers for the ATS arrived in 1941 with instructions that I report to a training centre in Wrexham, North Wales for 'Basic Training'. I travelled by train from Ludlow on a train so cramped, it was standing room only. As the day vanished so did our light because of the blackouts and it was impossible to see where we were.

The training centre was situated within the Royal Welsh Fusiliers' barracks. Although in the same compound, we occupied separate areas from the men.

On arrival we underwent a series of medical examinations and various anti viral injections, followed by our kit issue. The standard kit issue consisted of:

- A khaki cap
- A khaki skirt and tunic
- Khaki shirts, collars and ties
- Bras, vests, knickers, stockings
- Shoes (beetle crushers!)
- Tooth brush and shoe brushes
- Pyjamas
- Great coat and rain coat
- Gas mask
- Shoulder bag
- Disposable sanitary towels

I enjoyed wearing uniform (even though it wasn't a very good fit); it was something to be proud of. A collar and tie was a totally new experience for me and the collar left a red painful mark on my neck. Learning to tie the tie took ages – but we helped each other out. The khaki knickers were so long for me that they either showed below my knees or if pulled up, the waist line ended under my armpits. Overall our kit was pretty rough but it served its purpose.

We were housed in wooden huts made up of basic standard military equipment – functional but not very comfortable. This was to be our home for the 6 week basic training as we were marched, paraded and assessed for intelligence and trade assignments by female drill sergeants.

Pay for a Private was ten shillings (50p) per week, which

doesn't sound much but out of it we went to the cinema and were able to buy toiletries – sometimes. There was, of course, a shortage of everything. Later, at Bletchley Park I recall being able to buy one small bar of chocolate per week from the NAAFI.

Charlotte Vine-Stevens, 1945 © Charlotte Webb

Life in barracks was a complete culture shock for me. Girls from all walks of life and backgrounds rubbed shoulders, all learning to work as a team, all with a common purpose – to serve our country. It seems minor in the chaos of our lives, but the biggest shock came from viewing the social behaviour displayed by the girls and in particular the varied standard of table manners. Until that point I had naively believed everyone had lived as I had.

Some of my tasks were also an education. I remember I was given the unpleasant task of looking for lice – something I had never heard of. Those of the new recruits who were found to have lice were bandaged in paraffin-soaked head scarves but with so many girls living in close quarters the battle of head lice was not so easily won.

The Gas Mask was heavy, compared with the civilian models and had to be carried at all times. I particularly remember the gas mask drill where we were taken to a small room while wearing our gas masks and a small amount of gas was released. We were then ordered to remove our gas masks and everyone was instantly convulsed by coughing and spluttering as the gas entered our lungs. It taught us the importance of carrying our gas masks at all times, taking gas warnings seriously and obeying procedure without question.

The quiet life in rural Herefordshire and home schooling had not equipped me for anything in particular beyond being able to communicate in reasonable colloquial German, which I learned through Mother and a number of Swiss and German 'au pairs' during my early years. My abandoned college course had only equipped me for running a family home so I arrived in Wrexham with no true understanding of what my skills were. It was an interesting time to find out just exactly what I could put my mind to.

I enjoyed the experience of my basic training and by the end I waited with trepidation to see which trade I would be assigned to. Every recruit was assessed and allocated a trade but not for me a posting as a cook, orderly, signal operator, driver, radar operator. No, I was ordered to an address in London which entailed an overnight journey in a very crowded train. I rolled up my great coat for a pillow and lay in the corridor for most of the journey. Of course there were no lights and it was difficult to see those around me. What a relief to arrive at Euston at 6.30a.m., deposit my kit bag in the Left Luggage office, walk to Piccadilly and have breakfast at Lyons Corner House. Porridge was on the menu, but it did not taste as good as the brand I was used to – having been cooked overnight in our Aga.

It had been four years since the whirlwind tour of London in 1937. It seems ironic to me now that my first visit to the capital was as part of my journey to pre-war Germany, where I had received so much hospitality and my second visit, as part of my duty in the fight against Germany. London was still very grand despite the bomb damage of 1940. By today's standards there were hardly any civilians and very little traffic.

When I arrived at Devonshire House in Piccadilly I still had no idea why I was there. I was interviewed in German by a very pleasant twinkly-eyed Army Major from the Intelligence Corps. The interview was short and he did not tell me why I had been ordered there or what was expected of me. I was asked how I would communicate with someone in Scotland to which I responded I would do so by telephone, in writing, by telegram or by courier. There were also general questions about my family but nothing about my time in Germany in 1937. It seemed a strange interview as there was no discussion of my skills. I suspect it was a test of my overall intelligence, language skills and reliability.

I had obviously passed the interview but still did not know what was going on. My orders were to go to Euston railway station and take a train to Bletchley in the Buckinghamshire countryside where I would be met. It may now seem strange that I just followed my instructions without knowing my final destination or the reason for the journey but it was what I was trained to do, and did so willingly without any trepidation.

I was given a rail warrant and sent on my way with no further instructions. I collected my kit and boarded the train to Bletchley. Where Bletchley was, I had no idea! Another ATS girl, Wynn Angell, who was fluent in French, had also been directed to Bletchley. We began to talk and found we were heading to the same place. The train journey passed while listening to Wynn's description of her dramatic journey to Bletchley - she had recently escaped from Belgium (where the Germans had already taken over) and once in England she had joined the ATS, keen to contribute to the war effort.

It was late by the time the train pulled up at Bletchley Station. Together we were taken to a civilian 'Billet' in Bradwell. It was a council house with three bedrooms already housing a family of four. Tired and hungry Wynn and I were directed to the room which would be ours, only to find we had to share a bed! Despite our embarrassment, sheer exhaustion won over and we slept.

CHAPTER FIVE

BLETCHLEY PARK

Pencil drawing of Bletchley Park © Mark Pettifer, 2007

It was September 1941 and I awoke in a strange bed, in a strange house with absolutely no idea the reason why I was there. After getting ready Wynn and I walked to the end of the drive and, as instructed, caught the coach transporting thirty or so people to Bletchley. We travelled the five miles to a destination which was still unknown to us. I still had no concept of where I was once I arrived at Bletchley Park. It was a large ugly house, surrounded by a well guarded perimeter.

The bus drove us along the drive to the mansion where we were dropped off and led into the small office next to the library where we were given the Official Secrets Act to read and swear we would abide by. I remember it was a vast document to read on the spot but its seriousness was very clearly pointed out to us. In short, that any and all information we read or heard within Bletchley Park must NEVER be talked about outside the department we were assigned to and not for 30 years after the end of hostilities.

An Army Captain oversaw our induction and his emphasis of the implications of breaking our silence remains with me today. There were degrees of punishment to fit the severity of any betrayal – the most serious being the death penalty. Looking at the gun lying beside the Captain, I realised the extreme seriousness of the duty with which I had been entrusted.

I felt at a loss as to how I should conduct myself. I took the decision that the only way forward was to say nothing outside of my office. As time went on I found that the new found reserve influenced my personality in that I was and still am more discreet about my own life. I found, as many of us did, our social conversations were flippant and inconsequential.

On that first day, it became clear that no-one could be told where I was – not even my parents. Letters were to be addressed to a Post Office Box number in London. I could phone out but not receive calls. This was totally unexpected and came as a real shock - while at Bletchley I was 'cut off'. However, we could travel about on leave days and I did go home from time to time, or have a day in London, Oxford, Cambridge or Bedford etc. My family readily accepted my situation and never asked me any awkward questions. Dad was ex-Army and therefore knew better than to ask.

So, 'fate' had taken me to the Government Code and Cypher School (GC&CS) for the duration of the Second World War. I was one of thousands drawn from our universities, our three services, civil servants and local men and women, all working on the painstaking process of breaking the various codes in German, Italian and Japanese in order to find out those countries' military moves and intentions.

WORK DUTIES

Bletchley, with its nine to ten thousand employees drawn from all three services, and civil servants, male and female was a unique organisation and a unique experience. It is probably fair to say that every class of people in this country was represented. But we were a team of trustworthy individuals who had an important job to do – even though at the time we did not know the full story and 'small fry' like me did not ask!

Promotion at Bletchley was automatic – there were no tests or interviews, our rank progressed so that our pay was comparable with the civilians.

After signing the Official Secrets Act I was taken up the stairs to Major Tester's department. Wynn was taken somewhere else, possibly one of the huts but we never discussed it. I was put straight to work.

My first duties were in Major Ralph Tester's department which had rooms in the Mansion above the Ballroom. The four rooms were fairly small, and had possibly been servants' quarters in the time of the Leon family. I shared a small room with three men, which contained a desk for each of us and an open fire as the only heating source. The fire was only used at night but even then, we found there was insufficient fuel to last through the colder nights. The room was rather claustrophobic, but we could see out over Hut 4 at the side of the mansion.

My duties were registering the Morse code messages as they came in from the 'Y' (signal) stations by their hundreds, either by dispatch rider or teleprinter. The registering of each message by date and call sign order was necessary for the decoders and translators to make quick reference. This was the only part of the message 'in the clear'. The rest was simply groups of five letters or figures. The information was carefully recorded on index cards, which were placed in shoe boxes on the desk. I found this rather boring at the time but realise that all the less interesting tasks were vital to the whole process of codebreaking.

After registration, the messages were decoded, translated, transcribed and assessed according to urgency and then forwarded appropriately i.e. the Prime Minister, Commanders in the field or both. We worked a shift pattern 8am-4pm, 4pm-midnight, midnight-8am. Sounds easy – but it was tiring!

Major Tester was a nice, fatherly man who spoke perfect German and was engaged in translating at a very high level, particularly as he was also an expert in idiomatic German. After working with him for some time, he gave me a little test to see if my German was good enough to help with translations – he gently told me it was NOT!! (At least I tried). So I continued with three others to sort and register the Morse code messages which came in vast quantities each day. It is said that many thousand a day were received – so there must have been another department which also registered them, we three could not have coped with the lot.

Extract from Charlotte Vine-Stevens' Pay Book showing her posting in No. 4 Intelligence School, (4IS) the covername given by the War Office to the Military Section at Bletchley Park © Charlotte Webb (also see Appendix 2)

In a very small room next to mine worked a retired Colonel Thompson who had served with my Uncle Rex Vine-Stevens in the Royal Marine Engineers. Colonel Thompson recognised my name and introduced himself.

I remember two of the three men I shared an office with – Tubby Rootes, A Company Sergeant Major and a chap named Le Mesurier, whose Christian name I do not recall. This is not unusual as we were generally referred to by our surnames. However, later on Christian names were used more commonly.

Every Wednesday morning Tubby Rootes relieved the most unpleasant twenty minutes set aside for the weekly gas mask drill. His rendition of 'In the Mood' with his gas mask on made the most hilarious bubbling sound.

In 1943/1944 when it became necessary to increase the

number of staff in the Japanese Section I was transferred there in the newly built Block F (now demolished). My duties there included paraphrasing translated Japanese messages. My section head was C.J.W (Don) Parkin, a Foreign Office official.

It was considered a precaution to paraphrase messages which we had picked up and decoded, so that if when we were passing on details of impending Japanese troop movements in Burma and they picked up our transmissions giving details of an impending counter attack, they could not be certain that we had broken their codes.

The paraphrased messages were sent in an inner and outer envelope, each with a coded address. I believe they were taken to a destination by despatch riders, but I did not know to whom.

TABULATED EXAMPLES OF TRANSLATED MESSAGES AND THE PARAPHRASED VERSION	
Translated Intercepted Message	**Paraphrased Version of the Message**
Troops of 3rd Battalion will be moved to attach Kohima in 3 days time.	Expect Kohima to be attacked 3 days from now by battalion strength.
The road between Meiktila and Kohima will be blocked on Monday to Thursday by tanks.	Road from Meiktila to Kohima to be out of use for 4 days due to tanks assembling.
Division stationed Meiktila will attack from East – Mon May 1st .	Expect attack early May, to west, probably Jap division 10.

I enjoyed getting my teeth into more 'meaty' work within the Japanese Section, but I appreciate how crucial to the process my previous task of registration was, even if it was dull.

The Japanese Section in Block F was a large section made up of four offices served by a central passageway and comprised of army and civilian personnel (ATS and Intelligence Corps staff) working twenty four hours over three shifts. There were 3 ATS girls in my office and the change from working with men for 3 years went off without a hitch. Our office was terribly cramped; we had a desk each with a typewriter and the only other furniture I recall is some sort of filing cabinet that had to be locked at the end of each shift.

Don Parkin was in the office next to mine. He was a very kindly man, easy to get on with and made working for him very pleasant. His wife was a WAAF sergeant and she would often call into the office for him. She must have also worked in the Japanese Section because coming to call for him from a different section would have been a breach of the security rules.

'HOORAY FOR THE WEEKLY PAY PARADE'

Pay Parade - a welcome relief from the daily grind **and** a top up for our finances.

As a humble Private 10s 6d was the rate for a week and then more once one was promoted. To get this anticipated weekly pay we entered a hut near the Mansion (I remember that it was near Hut 4, but is no longer there). The easy chatter and laughter between fellow members of the ATS ended at the entrance to the hut. Pay Parade was a serious and very formal business.

We assembled in a line in alphabetical order 'at ease' facing the office sitting at a table with our pay packets containing the appropriate amount of cash. In the silence of the room we waited and as our name was called we stood to attention, marched up to the officer and saluted. Next we transferred our pay books from our left hand to our right and gave them to the officer to record the pay for that day. Finally we picked up the money with our right hand, transferred to our left, saluted, did an about turn and marched out of the room.

We had to attend even if we off duty, but I can't recall how it worked when we were on night duty.

RECREATION

Duties permitting, there were plenty of recreational activities to take part in, such as a drama group, gramophone club, a madrigal group or Bach choir concerts under Herbert Murrill, who was a professional singer and was employed by one of the radio stations after the war) and concerts given by the RAF Griller String Quintet. Towards the end of the war, after 600 American servicemen had joined Bletchley Park, dances were laid on, with American refreshments which were, of course, a great treat.

The easiest way to get around was by bicycle. Unfortunately, mine was stolen at Bletchley Park during the war. I contacted the Military Police but was more or less told to go away as it wasn't a priority. I often wonder who took it. Good luck to them - it was a very basic contraption with an uncomfortable seat, a temperamental wheel and no bell.

Charlotte Webb looking for her long lost bicycle, 2013
© Bletchley Park Research

Lectures were often given that were free to attend. The park grounds also formed part of our recreation time. If it was fine weather we would sit by the lake or walk around the grounds. One year there was heavy snowfall and people could be seen ice skating on the lake. Once I had left the billet in Loughton and went into the military camp on Shenley Road, there was also darts and my favourite game, table tennis. There was even a bar, but very rarely anything to drink.

Although we did not have lots of free time the varied social occasions made it easy to find new friends among others who were well aware of not being able to talk about our work. Things were a little trickier with friends outside of the park!

Soon after I arrived at Bletchley my parents introduced me to a handsome Canadian, who served in the Royal Canadian Air Force (RCAF). He was based at Biggin Hill, a large aerodrome in the south of England and we would meet in London and see shows and enjoy restaurant meals. One time he decided to surprise me and turned up in London unannounced and without the knowledge that the PO Box number on our correspondence was not my actual address. He arrived to be faced with nothing more than the post box system.

He was fun to be with and I enjoyed his company but the relationship did not last. Although he was keen to pursue our relationship I did not feel sufficient spark to tempt me with the possibility of going to Canada once the war was over.

I became good friends with a Junior Commander, Helen Mary Little through our mutual enjoyment of music. We attended concerts at the Park, which were held in the canteen.

The canteen was just outside the park gates on Wilton Avenue and depending on the shift pattern I either ate there or at my billet. Food and board was paid for by the army so my pay could be used for toiletries, cinema and chocolates depending on what was available in town.

When I was billeted in Loughton with the Foxley family, eating there was far more preferable to eating in the canteen. There were five family members and 3 of us ATS girls all adding to the rations. The family also had a fruit and vegetable garden so there was plenty of food for us all.

Once, while at Loughton, I remember oversleeping. In my rush to catch the bus to the Park I ran down the stairs without my skirt and had to make a hasty and embarrassed retreat to hide the army issue khaki knickers. Luckily the bus had other village collections to make so once dressed, I walked the fifteen minute journey to the A5 to catch the bus at its next stop.

Once the military camp was built to house the increasing workforce, I moved along with many others to the camp on Shenley Road, situated north of the park. The camp came under the command of Lt. Col. Fillingham. It was made up of a series of huts designed to house about eighteen people but ended up with thirty beds to each one. They were built from breeze blocks and bitumen floors. Each hut had two stoves fuelled with wood and coke. They were very difficult to fire and caused an awful lot of smoke, which was almost worse than being cold! The chimneys were unprotected so we had to be very careful not to touch them. Because of these hazards, we often didn't light the stoves – instead we would have a hectic game of table tennis just before bed time and rush under the covers while our circulation was at its best.

We had three square palliasses each. In order to reduce the risk of falling into the gaps onto bare boards as they slithered and slipped during the night, we sacrificed a blanket in which to 'parcel' the palliasses.

Food was served in the mess, which was mixed so men and women ate together. The separate ablutions block had concrete floors and duck boards to stand on by each wash basin. We were only allowed four inches of water in our baths!

The camp had a perimeter fence but in the hot summer we would take our bedding into a nearby field to cool down. Once or twice we even slept there and made a hasty retreat back to our huts in the morning. We never got caught, but then our hut was the last hut nearest the field.

Post War Ordnance Survey Map of Bletchley © Crown Copyright

CHAPTER SIX

WASHINGTON DC

It was May 1945, the European war was over but there was still work to be done. The war with Japan was still in progress and our attention was moved towards sending staff to work in Delhi.

Along with twenty others, I reported to Company Office for an interview to assess my suitability for Delhi. I was selected but I somehow knew I would not be going even though my name was on the deployment list. I had a strange premonition, which has not been uncommon in my life, convincing me that Delhi was not to be my next destination.

The next day Don Parkin, Head of the Japanese Section, told me I would be going to Washington. In fact, I would be working in the newly constructed Pentagon building. I felt both honoured and excited especially as I was the only member of the ATS to be posted there – a humble staff sergeant!

Before heading across the ocean I had to complete a very important mission – to the hairdresser. In those days it wasn't a simple operation. In fact I had to travel to Oxford an upmarket hairdresser managed by two Cypriot men. It was worth the time and the expensive 4 guineas price tag for a perm that lasted throughout my time in the humid conditions of America. You can see the perm on the front cover of this book! With a new hairstyle I was ready for another journey.

After a short embarkation leave I travelled to Euston Station and took the bus to the War Office Holding Unit, ATS, 12 Radnor Place, London located near Hyde Park. The unit was effectively a holding camp for army staff waiting for deployment outside the country. Notably, Winston Churchill's youngest daughter, Mary Spencer-Churchill, was stationed at the unit towards the end of the European war as an ATS Junior Commander.

Prime Minister Winston Churchill of Great Britain, accompanied by his daughter, Mary Churchill. NARA - 198765. Licensed under Public domain via Wikimedia Commons

It was Whitsun 1945 and the first holiday since the outbreak of war that people were able to visit London without the fear of bombings. This visit was no holiday for me: the officer responsible for my movement order was on weekend leave and the relevant envelope lay unopened on her desk. I had no option but to wait at the holding centre, sleeping in basic accommodation while I waited for further instructions.

Following a telephone call to Don Parkin to explain why I was still in London, he quickly arranged for me to be seen by another department in the War Office. The problem was soon resolved and I was sent on a train to Poole to catch a Sunderland flying boat to Baltimore.

The journey gave me time to reflect on the advice of one of the officers at the holding unit. 'Remember, as a member of HM Forces you are an Ambassador for Great Britain, so behave appropriately.' Apart from the occasional Mint Julip drink at parties, I was very appropriately behaved.

Getting onto the Sunderland flying boat meant a very choppy ride in a small boat from the harbour and then unceremoniously clambering onto the Sunderland's wings to get on board.

This was my first flight and I was extremely scared of taking to the skies in such uncertain times. Who knew what would be waiting for us up beyond the clouds? I was also unnerved by the anonymity of the civilian clothes worn by my fellow passengers. I was in uniform, but the other passengers (all male) were wearing civilian clothes, which made me more nervous because I feared they might ask me what I was doing and where I was going. Fortunately, none of them spoke to me. I must have been a most unattractive travelling companion as I was quite unable to stop my sickness, even though the pilot kindly gave me some pills: they didn't help!

The first stop was somewhere in Ireland to refuel and eat. It was dark and I felt too ill to eat or enquire where we were. We climbed back aboard the Sunderland to find the seating had been rearranged so that we could lie down and sleep. We soon took off again and continued to fly due east for what seemed to be an endless sleepless night. Finally, we came down through a beautiful morning mist to land at Botwood, on the Canadian island of Newfoundland.

We looked out over a vast expanse of fir trees as we ate breakfast at the airport. I was amazed to see bacon and eggs on the menu and found it ignited my appetite. I happily ate the bacon and eggs as well as trying Grape-Nuts, which is a breakfast cereal that neither contains grapes nor nuts but is actually made from wheat and barley. The breakfast worked wonders at easing my travel sickness and finally I was able to enjoy our flight south west over the United States of America to Baltimore.

Feeling weak and tired I was relieved to get out of the Sunderland at last. Captain John Burrows from my section, at Bletchley Park who had selected me to go out to Washington, met me at the airport and escorted me on the final leg of my journey to Washington DC. Years later I asked John why he had chosen me for Washington. He simply answered 'because I thought it was a good idea'.

I was relieved when he took me straight to my billet at the Cairo Hotel on 16th and Q in Washington to finally get some sleep before starting work the next day. I quickly found my room, which I was to share with Pip Wallace, another ATS girl who came from Hull. I didn't know it then on that first night, or was too tired to care, but the hotel was very uncomfortable and did not have air-conditioning. The oppressive 100 degree heat, high humidity and constant battle with the thriving cockroaches in my room were the only drawbacks of my five month stay in the capital city. Pip turned out to be a very good cockroach catcher, which was a good thing since every night we had to kill as many as possible before we could go to bed wrapped in bath towels to combat the sticky heat.

John Burrows & Charlotte Vine-Stevens, Washington 1945
© Charlotte Webb

The next morning I dressed in my uniform, quickly realising that I would be perspiring from the moment I did up the last button of the woven jacket designed for British weather. Before long I was issued with a light Canadian summer uniform which included nylons that felt so light compared to those issued at home, but on that first day, I had to endure my own heavy kit.

I left the hotel and caught the designated bus travelling to my new place of work, The Pentagon. Travelling for the first time like a wide eyed sightseer, I gazed out of the window marvelling at the city as we took the 20 to 30 minute journey over the Arlington Bridge and Potomac River into the state of Virginia, where The Pentagon is sited. Although technically it is in Arlington, Virginia, The Pentagon is addressed as Washington DC (District of Colombia). It was on these bus journeys that I experienced segregation for the first time - the African American travellers were confined to the back of the bus.

The Pentagon, 1945. Image taken from a promotional brochure bought at
The Pentagon in 1945. © Department of Defence
(also see Appendix 3 for more from the brochure)

The enormity of The Pentagon building is hard to describe. Compared with today there was lots of open space around it so it stood proudly out of the landscape. Situated over five floors, the offices started on the first floor above the ground level car park. The bus drove straight into the car park where I was met by John Burrows who escorted me to a meeting with the Section Head.

The Pentagon was enormous – a far bigger operation than I had experienced at Bletchley Park. The Pentagon was built quickly to cope with the growing demands of the growing government War Department. On 15 January 1943 the vast site spanning over 34 acres was complete.

From the car park escalators took the thirty two thousand workers, who passed through the building over a twenty four hour period into a vast busy concourse. The concourse had shops, a bank, medical centre and church. Security was tight and access to the concourse was only granted upon the presentation of your pass to the US Army personnel stationed at each access point. The same procedure was then followed outside your office and it was checked every day without fail. I remember I was friendly with one of the American girls who checked the passes and one day I asked in frustration if she really needed to check my details. She still checked my details and did so every day that I worked in the building.

Colonel O'Connor was the American Section Head whose staff included John Burrows, James Pope-Hennessey (later, Queen Mary's biographer), me and others from other US and UK services. I seem to recall that the majority of general staff were women and we worked in a large open plan office accessed via a ramp from the main concourse.

A concourse inside The Pentagon, 1945. Image taken from a promotional brochure bought at The Pentagon in 1945. © Department of Defence

I had a desk and typewriter where I was tasked with paraphrasing intelligence reports derived from the intercepted Japanese communications from Burma. Although the four year Burma campaign was effectively at an end by the time I arrived in Washington, the Japanese forces did not surrender until the end of August 1945. The process of paraphrasing was identical to my duties at Bletchley and although I don't remember exactly the contents, I do recall there was a constant flow of signals passing between Japanese forces which kept me busy between my work hours of 9am to 5pm.

There were many British personnel on duty in Washington and we were well integrated with our American allies. We were required to visit the British Embassy and sign the visitor's book. By way of acknowledgment we all received visiting cards from

HM Ambassador and the Countess of Halifax. I still have mine.

Sometimes my duties involved being a Special Courier of secret papers from one department to another within Washington. To me, that was scary. I remember clutching the precious documents to my person and was greatly relieved having delivered them without incident.

At work I often took lunch with my American colleagues and we had the choice of where to eat as food was served in canteens as well as outside in the five acre open air area in the courtyard at the building's centre. This was the area where General Dwight Eisenhower drove round in a tank when he returned from Europe after the end of hostilities. Despite its size, the temperature of the central area took your breath away in contrast to the cool air-conditioned building so I preferred to eat my lunch inside.

Lunch-time in the courtyard at The Pentagon, 1945. Image taken from a promotional brochure bought at The Pentagon in 1945.
© Department of Defence

Of all the food I ate, I mostly remember the salads which included watermelon. Although common place today they were a complete luxury to me after all those years of rationing. Rationing was minor in comparison with the level I experienced at home. However, there was some rationing of meat, which was exchanged for small tokens.

There were no catering facilities at The Cairo Hotel so all my meals were taken in cafes or restaurants. I paid forty four dollars a month for my room and I was paid an extra five dollars a day for food which was ample for covering my eating expenses. Food was not scarce; as soon as you sat down in the booth at a restaurant a waitress would bring out a jug of water and large lettuce leaf piled with cottage cheese to eat while you waited for the main course. I remember that you could deposit a nickel in a slot and select a record to be played within the booth.

Off duty I mostly mixed with British friends, either to eat out, go to cocktail parties at the flats of those fortunate to have them, concerts or the occasional visit to the ballet. Even in those days we were advised not to go about unescorted in the evenings. Our chaps were very helpful in this and always made sure we were seen back to our billets. I wore civilian clothes when off duty, which were cheap to buy but did not seem to be made of the same quality as those I had at home. Not that I minded, as again it was a pleasure to explore the department stores and have choices that were not available in the time of frugal rationing at home.

I got on well with my roommate Pip: we had formed a strong bond over our cockroach annihilations. Pip had short dark hair and a pretty, friendly face and had a fun personality. We only met up in the evenings back at the hotel as she did not work in The Pentagon. I know she was a Private in the ATS but I did not know what she did in Washington.

In the autumn I did manage to get away from the city for a weekend with my American friend (who checked my pass each morning at the office door). We travelled by train to her family home near Providence in Rhode Island. Again the contrast with the train journeys I had taken in England was remarkable – there were no blackouts, no crowding or sleeping on the floor. We did have an uncomfortable situation with a drunken GI pestering us, but the train guard soon moved him so we were able to enjoy our journey in peace. I remember how beautiful the countryside looked in the rich autumn colours and the fields of ripening corn. We spent a fabulous weekend roasting marshmallows on the barbecue and taking a tour by car to explore a landscape untouched by war.

At the end of the war with Japan, I was working in a British Joint Services Mission office and there met Commander Denniston's daughter, Margaret, known as 'Y'. We became friends and the last time we met was in 2005 just before she died. I do miss her.

On the morning of 6 August 1945 the atomic bomb was dropped on Hiroshima. The authorities intercepted a message indicating that Japan would never surrender and the decision was made to take the action that would finally turn the tide of war. On the 9 August 1945 a second bomb was dropped on Nagasaki. I will never forget hearing the news. Everyone in Washington (and no doubt the rest of the USA) 'went crazy'

– continuous blare of car horns and tearing around the city, shouting and waving. I joined a crowd who thronged around the White House calling 'We want Harry,' (Harry Truman who was President of the USA at the time).

I didn't truly understand the impact the bomb would have on Japan nor the lasting effects of radiation on future generations. At the end of a long war, it meant we were winning and on 14 August 1945 Japan finally surrendered.

Up to that point food had been rationed in the States, although not as rigidly as it was in UK. Steaks were difficult to come by, BUT on the day the bombs were dropped, steaks appeared in the restaurants as if by magic! The celebrations went on all night; such excitement and the noise from hundreds of car horns drowning everything else.

N.B. We were allowed to use our Washington addresses. I imagine my parents were relieved to know where I was after the long time at Bletchley Park where we not at liberty to tell them.

CHAPTER SEVEN

BACK TO BLETCHLEY

The war with Japan was finally at an end and the world was once again returning to a peace. It was October 1945 and time for the British Forces in Washington to return home. While waiting for my movement order I moved to a building near the White House to help out with general tidy up duties. Security was still tight and if I went shopping at lunchtime I had to show the guards everything I had bought, which could be embarrassing if it involved personal items. It was also time to hand back the light Canadian uniform and return to my official ATS uniform in preparation for the return to England. I managed to hang onto the light stockings, which caused much envy when I finally returned home.

Those last days held opportunities to do some shopping to buy lots of clothes and gifts for my parents. I filled my two issue kit backs and ended up obtaining a further two kit bags, which seemed a good idea until I had to carry a bag under each arm and one in each hand upon arrival in New York.

It was 5 October 1945 and I was to be in charge of a few

other ATS girls for the duration of the journey to England. We travelled on an English cruise ship, Aquitania, which had been requisitioned as a troop ship. It was in a rough, battered state and even though the travelling conditions were little more than basic, it was hard to dampen my excitement at going home.

On arrival in New York we were told the Stevedores (porters) were on strike, meaning we were stuck in New York. However, it gave us the opportunity to see something of New York, including a production of 'The Importance of Being Earnest' by some local nuns who sounded more English than we did – it was hilarious. I also went to the ballet, "Ballet Russe Highlights", choreographed by Leonide Massine. It was a collection of short ballet highlights, including a memorable one titled "The Dentist". The furious rain prevented me from really taking in the sights but the unexpected stay in New York was very enjoyable and was made possible by the additional pay allowance of seven dollars per day (we received five dollars in Washington).

Eventually, we were on board, but having to carry our own luggage. I spent most of the first two days sitting on deck enjoying the glorious weather. Despite the greater feelings of relaxation, it was impossible not to have thoughts of unexploded sea mines. The Atlantic turned nasty and for the remaining three days to Southampton I was very sick and stayed below in rather basic conditions. It was a great relief to disembark! The MPs at Southampton kindly took me and the other ATS girls through a side door avoiding Customs and put us on a train for London where I felt relieved to finally arrive at the holding unit at Radnor Place. In my excitement to be back I thought of calling on my friend Angela Lenton, so rushed into her office, only to find myself face to face with Mary Spencer-Churchill, the Prime Minister's daughter, a Junior Commander in the ATS. She smiled sweetly as I backed out in embarrassment saying 'Very sorry Ma'am'.

From Radnor Place I was sent back to Bletchley, where I arrived as they were shredding paper and dismantling machinery. I have no memory of how long I was there waiting for a new posting, I just remember the atmosphere one gets after everyone has gone home from a party or a feeling of emptiness after packing a house up before a move.

My stay must have been only for one or two nights at the Shenley Road Camp, where I remember eating a meal. I was not required to help the few people left to pack up the site so I felt a little lost and, it is sad to say, it was almost an anticlimax in comparison to the bustle and focus which had filled the place during the war years.

For me, the war was over. I had one last night at Bletchley before I was posted to East Grinstead to wait for discharge from the Army (demob). My demob group to come up in February 1946 and finally I could go home and spend time with my family.

PASS

ARMY FORM B.295

REGT. A.T.S.

No. 782948   Rank S/Cpl

Name Vine-Stevens E.E.

has permission to be absent from his unit

from there 18 Nov' 45 to 2000 12 Nov 45

M Morrowburne

Commanding

STAMP (pads of 100)
(with unit or formation identification
number or letter blanked out).

INTELLIGENCE CORPS

1. From London District	4. Reporting Centre	7 Ration Card Issued
2. To London	5. Eire/N. Ireland Destination	8. For use of C.M.P.
	Berkeley	
	Valid only with A.B.64	
3. Through London	6. Nearest Hospital or Medical Unit	9

* Items not applicable to be deleted and initialled by issuing officer vide Leave Manual, 1943, and any
subsequent amendments.
(P.T.O.)

CHAPTER EIGHT

POST WAR YEARS

Armed with a 'nest egg' of £52 and clothing coupons, I went back to the family smallholding, Ryecroft, to help out. The war years must have been a great strain on my parents, as it was for thousands of others of that age group. There was a collective air of sadness for the loss of loved ones, loneliness and uncertainty. Not to mention the daily struggle caused by food and fuel shortages.

My war years were relatively comfortable and interesting. Bletchley Park was for me the next best thing to a University – exploring a new found independence and living amongst a cross-section of interesting people. In my view, it was a unique establishment and a unique experience. I am sure such a gathering could never be repeated!

Life moved on and so did I. The government paid for my six months secretarial course in London from late 1946 to Easter 1947. A dreadful winter – everywhere was frozen up, and the food and fuel shortage had not eased. Some of my fellow students fainted from the cold. I had dared to attend in a pair of Army issue trousers (dyed plum) and was sent for by the head. I was given a strict telling-off for appearing in such garb, which she described as 'quite unsuitable for young gentlewomen'. I pleaded with her, reminding her that travelling on an unheated train to and from Croydon each day warranted some protection. I got away with it on the understanding that the minute the weather improved, a skirt would be worn!

Charlotte Vine-Stevens 1947

We were well taught in shorthand, typing, a language of our choice (I took Spanish), how to write business letters and all the etiquette rules in connection with invitations and replies. We also received some guidance in stock market dealings (way over my head!) I came away with my only qualification - a RSA 1st class in Typing.

Cousin Rosemary Harris was on the same course and sailed through everything with top marks as she always did, and with her degree (BA) in, I think, Latin and Greek, she soon had a job as Personal Assistant to the Head man at the NIRD (National Institute of Research Dairies) at Reading University where she remained for 47 years and was awarded an MBE for her work there.

Adjusting to the post-war years was difficult. Many had had their education/training interrupted. Food shortages and rationing was with us until 1953. For me, those initial post war years held another obstacle. Due to my obligations under the Official Secrets Act, I was not allowed to tell any prospective employer what I had been doing for the previous four or five years. Luckily, the then Head of Ludlow Grammar School had been at Bletchley himself so I had no difficulty in getting in there on the office staff. It was definitely a case of 'who you know' as distinct from 'what you know'.

Then by chance, because of my continued friendship with John and Margaret Borthwick which had begun in 1946 when I lived with Margaret's Aunt and Uncle Hancock whilst attending the secretarial course, I stumbled on a job with Messrs Williams & Williams, Metal Window manufacturers in Chester where John Borthwick was Managing Director. I was employed by Mr Tom Sarl-Williams as part of a team of five secretaries and dealt, mainly, with Staff Pensions.

There, I met another employee June Solloway, who had also been at Bletchley and we became good friends (and are to this day) and through her husband, who was a member of the 4th Battalion, the Cheshire Regiment – TA, I became an Officer of 321 (Cheshire Battalion) WRAC (TA).

Charlotte Vine-Stevens in Territorial Army uniform, mid 1950s
© Charlotte Webb

Mr Sarl-Williams was in favour of the TA and readily gave me time off to attend the annual TA camps (with pay). We shared the Drill Hall in Volunteer St Chester with the Cheshire Regiment and were even welcome in their Officers' Mess. It was jolly crowd of men – mostly local Solicitors, Land agents, etc. So the social life was good – lots of cocktail parties, dances, etc., and the great occasion when Her Majesty the Queen presented new Colours to the 4th and 7th Battalions on the Chester racecourse in 1957 followed by a splendid Ball which went on till 4am.

In Autumn 1959 I was invited to take the position of PSO (Permanent Staff Officer) to 321 (Ches) Bn. WRAC.TA, with the rank of Captain, Adjutant to the Commanding Officer Major Margaret Southern, which I did and stayed there until the re-organisation of the T.A. in 1961 when 319, 320 & 321 Battalions were amalgamated and the HQ set up in Southport. It was all very sad and I hated Southport.

Mummy visited me there: she was very ill and died a few weeks later in Hereford General Hospital. I was in Scotland at Camp near Gleneagles, but managed to get to the hospital in time to be with her before she died. However, I doubt if she knew I was there with Daddy and Margaret.

We were all shattered and saddened by Mummy's death – I had no idea how to come to terms with life without her and was not helped by the new Commanding Officer's hard response to my tears: she said 'I didn't cry when my mother died'. Dad's distraught state convinced me to ask for a posting to Bristol which made it easier to get to Monkerton House, near Leominster, where Dad lived, if I was needed.

So eventually I moved to Bristol and was able to go by train to Leominster and give Dad a little moral support more easily. He was totally 'lost' without Mummy but insisted I should carry on with my life in the Army. Life does have to go on, we have no choice.

My years as a full-time TA Officer brought me into contact with people from all walks of life from the very humblest to the very highest in Society. I was apprehensive when faced with meeting the Duke and Duchess of Beaufort in the sixties. They were both very active in the Bristol area and the Duchess became our Honorary Colonel (71 Bristol Coy WRAC (TA)) and as such she visited our premises and the Mess and hosted the company at Badminton House for a training weekend. I slept in the Duke's old bedroom in a brass bedstead with a red silk bedspread. The walls were adorned with photos of his Eton days.

I need not have been afraid – the Duke and Duchess were very kind to us and easy to talk to. I will never forget the Duchess reminding me of the collective name for goldfinches and when she joined us at TA camp in Folkestone I asked her if she would like breakfast in bed and she replied, 'Oh no, Betty, thank you, I hate crumbs in bed!'

It was the Duchess who presented all our officers with a shield when the company was disbanded in 1966. Mine is proudly displayed in my hall above my 'Bletchley – Freedom of the Park' parchment.

At the other end of the scale were those I enlisted into the Regular WRAC and QARANC whilst working as a Recruiting Officer for the West Midlands from 1966-1969. I interviewed the applicants in Birmingham, Stoke-on-Trent (Hanley), Shrewsbury, Worcester, Hereford, Wolverhampton and Coventry – a very mixed bag of accents and attitudes, rich and poor, educated and not so. My time at Bletchley, Washington and the Army had given me the skills to communicate and engage with people from all backgrounds with respect and compassion. It is all those experiences that made me good at my job and I never forgot the value of discretion.

During that time I drove or was driven to the above towns from Birmingham on a weekly basis. So I have grown up with some of our major road developments, particularly the ring roads in Birmingham, the M5, 6 and 42. Driving was more of a pleasure then. Now it is so very hazardous; the volume of traffic and drivers' lack of consideration and sense of danger. My driving experience dates back to the late 1940s and includes some appalling weather conditions during the winters of 1963/4 and others.

I left the Army in September 1969 for a post as Area Secretary to the YWCA, which I had expected to ensure me a pension (The Army had not, because my commission was as a Territorial as distinct from a Regular Officer). The move turned out to be a disaster – I did not understand it and was most unhappy. However, Alfred and I had met in 1968 and Daddy was having trouble with his eyesight – two good reasons to leave the YWCA for happier times.

Alfred and I met on a chance encounter when I was looking for a garage to park my car at night in Shirley, West Midlands. Attracted to my uniform and shared wartime experiences, romance blossomed.

Alfred and I married on 18 July 1970 in Leominster on a lovely sunny day with a small party of family and friends in the garden of my father's home, Monkerton House, Stoke Prior. After that, Alfred and I, and dog Prince, motored to Yorkshire for a week.

Charlotte & Alfred Webb on their wedding day, 18 July 1970

We were destined to have only nine and a half years together; they were good years for me, very different being a wife and housewife after all the varied experiences of my previous life. We settled in a large but rather neglected house in Redditch, Worcestershire. Alfred restored our house into a comfortable home during a time that Redditch Town was undergoing massive development. We named the house 'Redwing' after seeing a Redwing bird land in the garden at Daddy's house just at the time we were trying to think of a name.

It was an irony that Alfred had survived the War in the Army (Guards Armoured Division) in Europe without a scratch to be diagnosed with hardening of the arteries in 1976 at the age of fifty seven.

The medics at the Queen Elizabeth Hospital did all they could to keep him alive but it was not to be and with hindsight, I think Alfred would have hated life as an amputee. I was shattered, of course, and it took me a long time to come to terms with life without him. Colin, Alfred's son from a previous marriage, and his family lived nearby and were a great comfort as were his other son's Ian, Pete and their families. I am very lucky to have shared happier times with my extended family.

Fortunately, my job at Birmingham Law Society was kept open for me and I returned to a job where I was happily employed for sixteen years as Administrative Secretary with a staff of twelve and being responsible to the Council. I also found new hobbies, including weekly Norwegian lessons given by Mrs Veslemoy Lunt, (whose husband Canon Ronald Lunt was head of King Edward's School, Birmingham).

The Norwegian lessons introduced me into another interesting mix of people – some with direct Norwegian connections, others, like me, just learning Norwegian and Norwegian culture, simply because we were interested. I learnt that Canon and Mrs Lunt met in Norway in the early days of the War when he was parachuted in with our Forces. I also met ex-Bletchley WREN, Joan Martin. Her son is married to a Norwegian and as the local choir master in Straume, near Bergen, brought the choir to Birmingham. We entertained them and made more friends. One of the families entertained me in Norway in 1992 and I still write to them at Christmas time.

Norway is beautiful and I'm glad I was able to speak a little Norwegian, as I felt those we came in contact with were pleased to hear some of the English making an effort! In my view, to say English is spoken everywhere you go is neither true nor the right attitude. We are lazy about learning other languages. It is a pity because this attitude means we miss out on so much. When people ask me 'Why Norwegian?' My reply is 'why not?' I find it fascinating although it's sometimes similarity to German gets me into trouble with Norwegians, who understandably prefer not to be associated with their one time invaders.

All through my working life since joining the ATS in August 1941, I have wondered how I would be 'rated' by others for not having had conventional schooling. 'PNEU Homeschool' doesn't always mean anything unless fully explained. However, I believe there are a small minority of people who were educated thus and like me, have managed to cope. Despite my worries and something of an inferiority complex, I succeeded in staying with various employments and generally 'holding my own' socially. To this day my heart always sinks when someone says 'Do you remember how it was at school?' But now I have plucked up courage to say 'No, I do not, because……'.

In September 1995 John Burrows, my colleague from Washington met again. This was after he retired from his post war job as a HM Inspector of Schools. He was made a CBE for his work in that department.

We had a wonderful time recalling our time with the British Army staff and the British Joint Services Mission in Washington. Remembering Colonel Colin Godley, US Army, Ruth Chaplin,

'Y' Denniston (Commander Denniston's daughter) and Oliver Berthoud, US Army. John died in 2008 aged 96.

I always embrace new experiences and the chance to practice my language skills. In 1999 I travelled from Heathrow to Santiago, which took twenty two hours. Admittedly there was a two-hour wait in Madrid but even so, it was a very long journey. I spent a month in Chile with my Cousin Josie and her husband Marco Garido in their beautiful home in Linderos, not far from Santiago. It was heaven. Around their bungalow there were beautiful trees and shrubs, and they grew every fruit and vegetable you can imagine. Two dogs (Daisy and Tyson), a horse, chickens and several acres of arable land. There was no street lighting so the night sky was perfect.

I felt a small earthquake one night but there was no damage. Walking in the foothills of the Andes with a crowd of local botanists was a particularly enjoyable day. Josie and I almost lost our way and had visions of spending the night surviving on water in the little stream nearby. However, we did found our way back and we went to see a cactus-type tree called Puya Chilensis.

The other nice time in Chile when Josie and I stayed with her friend Ilse in her holiday home in Valpariso, which is on the coast north of Linderos. The weather wasn't particularly good but it was quiet and we walked down to the see and saw lots of birds, some of which we would have found in England, but mostly native birds and I wasn't that good at identifying them. We spent two days there and afterwards went onto a fascinating garden centre. The difference between the rich and poor was very noticeable.

We went to Santiago by train but before we went Josie

warned me not to wear any jewelry which was in anyway valuable looking because it was too dangerous; people get robbed there as they do in other cities, but particularly in Santiago. In fact, when we were driving in on another occasion we had to stop at traffic lights, we were very careful to wind the windows up and make sure the doors were locked in case someone decided to try to take our valuables. We had a very nice day with Peter Oats and his wife, who took us to the Prince of Wales Country Club, a very posh place in a beautiful park in Santiago. Interestingly in the club there were commemorative plaques naming the women who had joined the ATS.

Peter Oats was involved with the South American British Legion and was therefore able to invite us to the Remembrance Sunday Service in November in the community church in Santiago. It was an impressive service at which the Ambassador of the USA and the British Ambassador both read Lessons during the service. Whilst it was mainly an English affair, they also sang the Chilean National Anthem in Spanish. Fortunately I knew enough Spanish to join in. Mr Oates read the Roll of Honour, remembering those who had fallen in World War 2.

The whole thing was very well done indeed. It was a service you would recognise in this country and I still have the programme. It is still is good to read it again. Along time ago but I still remember it clearly, we met the Oats family again - their daughter was employed by the British Embassy in Santiago.

We also had another day in Santiago with Marco's brother. While there I was thoroughly spoilt and everything was very pleasant indeed. The Chileans were very friendly and most spoke at least a little English. All in all the visit was lovely and I wish I could go back, but I think I'm too old for the flight now.

The country is very varied but mostly very beautiful and the wildflowers are absolutely lovely. While I was there it was October/November time (their Spring time) and there were masses of Californian Poppies in bloom. We had a lot of fun in Josie's house, particularly in the evening playing Scrabble. I was given a bottle of Amaretto to drink whilst playing. I think it was meant to help me score, but it didn't generally - apart from the last night when I made an enormous score, which I don't remember and was made quite by accident. They blamed my score on the strength of Amaretto.

I gained enormous confidence during 2005-2006, being thrown in at the deep end as Consort to my friend Jill Dyer, who was Chairman of our District Council and as such accompanied her to a great variety of Civil, Social and Business functions – about one hundred and fifty in all. A most interesting and rewarding experience AND a great privilege and honour. The highlight of the year was attending a garden party at Buckingham Palace on 19 July 2005. We were chauffeur-driven to London in the very luxurious official car and after a delicious lunch at the Goring Hotel in Beeston Place, we joined the crowd of nine and a half thousand people in the gardens at the rear of the Palace. Entrance is through the Palace, passing through the Ballroom. Everyone was obliged to verify their identity to the Palace guards by showing their passports, driving licences and a recent bill with full name and address. Afternoon tea consisted of beautifully presented sandwiches, cakes, ice-cream and iced coffee or other non-alcoholic beverages served by faultless young men and women in immaculate dress.

The guests were also very formally dressed – the ladies in

fabulous colours and of course, hats, the men in either military uniforms or morning dress, Chains of Office where appropriate. All added to the spectacle. Her Majesty the Queen, Prince Philip, the Duke of Kent, Prince Charles and the Duchess of Cornwall and the Duke of York mingled with the guests. Sadly, because of the numbers, we did not see Her Majesty at close quarters.

In recent years I have served on Wythall Parish Council as a Parish Councillor. I have been surprised and delighted that so many local groups, of one sort and another, invite me to speak to them about Bletchley Park, the National Codes Centre, my time there and its war time function. Giving these talks is most enjoyable for me and I am impressed by the amount of genuine interest in the subject.

It has not always been easy to talk about Bletchley Park, even after the veil of secrecy was lifted in July 1975. It took until about 1994 for me to open up about my experiences, when a friend suggested I give talks. My first talk was to his Probus Club and the talk was a hit. Since then I have talked to groups of about thirty to forty people but sometimes to in excess of a hundred people at a time. From retired people to a group of school children it seems that Bletchley Park has captured the imagination of the nation. I not only talk about Bletchley's past but its evolving future as a museum that is open to the public. New information regularly comes to light from veterans and documents released into the National Archives, further enriching Bletchley's story.

CHAPTER NINE

ONE BLETCHLEY EVENT LEADS TO ANOTHER

Since the launch of my book Secret Postings, I have been and still am, amazed at how much interest has been shown by my readers. The only criticism has been (so far), is that the story is too short.

The important outcome is that my story has engendered more interest in Bletchley Park, its role in World War 2 and its status as a World Class Museum and Archive.

Talks about Bletchley to various groups, clubs and schools has been and is very rewarding, mainly in the West Midlands. So far I have given over one hundred and I know many of the audiences have visited Bletchley Park as a result of hearing a little of its history from a veteran. Not only to learn about the purpose of the Government Code & Cypher School (GC&CS), but how its employees lived during the wartime conditions – our duties, recreation, living arrangements, friendships, marriages etc.

Being involved in the television programmes by invitation of Bletchley Park has been a great privilege and enormous fun. Links to some of the programmes and articles can be found at **www.bletchleyparkresearch.co.uk/authors-researchers/charlotte-webb.**

Charlotte Webb in the Bletchley Park bookshop 2013 © David Brown

Masterchef

I was one of six veterans who were chosen to be at a dinner prepared by the Masterchef team. The event was recorded in March 2012 and those who took part were asked to keep it a 'secret' until it was shown on television in September 2012. Our discipline to keep secrets came in handy once again. A taxi was arranged to and from, and after a champagne reception we moved into the Library when the dinner was served by the three Masterchef finalists.

The television progamme in addition to showing the chefs

at work gave a short history of each veteran's wartime role at Bletchley Park, with photographs taken at the time. Mine had omitted Major Ralph Tester's name, which I am sad about, as he was one of the important figures at the time. It was a memorable occasion, good food and much hilarity amoungst the guests. They always enjoy about hearing about the ATS khaki knickers!

William Hague

The Foreign Secretary, William Hague's visit to Bletchley Park when he announced government funding for the renovation of the huts was another occasion to which I was invited with six other veterans, Lord Briggs, Baroness Trumpington, Captain Jerry Roberts, Gwendoline Page, Jean Valentine and I were presented to Mr Hague who subsequently sent me a copy of his speech with a covering personal handwritten letter. How proud am I?

The audience included Sir Ian Lobban, the then Head of GCHQ, Gordon Corera, defence correspondent, and the Bletchley Park Trustees. William Hague was presented with an Enigma machine which I understand is now on display in the Foreign Office.

During refreshment breaks we veterans had a jolly reminiscing time even though we didn't know each other between 1939 and 1945. We still had much in common – there is a wonderful bond between us.

The Bletchley Park team headed by CEO Iain Standen are the best, so welcoming and interested in our wartime work there. I am sure that their hard work and genuine interest is just what is needed to keep Bletchley Park the World Class Heritage attraction it is fast becoming.

Bremont

Then came another totally unexpected invitation to be interviewed and tell my story to a super group of people from the Bremont company, who made a limited edition watch, called Codebreaker, which has within it tiny pieces of wood from Hut 6. The exciting aspect of this is that Bremont are donating part of the proceeds from the sale of the watches to Bletchley Park. Another wonderful team of people honoured me and Kerry Howard with an invitation to the launch of the Codebreaker watch. Hosted by Nick and Giles English, the co-founders of Bremont I along with other veterans (Captain Jerry Roberts, Ruth Bourne, Jean Valentine) were warmly welcomed by Serena Lechie and had a super time in the mansion.

Charlotte Webb & Nick English at the launch of the
Codebreaker Watch, 2013 © Bletchley Park Research

Much interest was shown by a great many guests about our wartime work. Men and women who were too young, some who were two or three generations younger than I am, who had only heard about World War 2 from their parents and grandparents.

I found it very warming to realise the respect with which they held us. It is difficult to imagine how anyone born after 1945 envisages how we lived through the war years and how those times influenced our way of life thereafter.

The evening was a wonderful, unique experience. I am very honoured to have been included.

Charlotte Webb and Ruth Bourne 2013© Bletchley Park Research

Great British Railway Journeys

Yes, there is more! Again an invitation from Bletchley Park to take part in the Great British Railway Journeys to be shown on television in early 2014. I drove down to Bletchley on a bitterly cold day and met by the media manager, Katherine Lynch and introduced to the Boundless team producer, Tom Richardson, whose father Philip I worked with as an Administrative Secretary to the Birmingham Law Society (such a small world). That was the preliminary session – perhaps to decide whether I would be suitable to be filmed with Michael Portillo? To my delight I was. So another trip to Bletchley Park, this time my friend Jill Dyer drove me and we gathered in the Ballroom where the stage was set for afternoon tea with Michael Portillo. He questioned me about my service at BP during World War 2. He was very nice and easy to talk to while we ate delicate sandwiches and drank endless cups of tea. I only wish he hadn't topped mine with so much milk as it was rather cool by the time I stopped talking long enough to drink it. Jill enjoyed hearing how such programmes are put together. While we waited for the broadcast during August 2013 I prepared to do another interview for a television programme by the BBC.

During the 2011 Reunion of ex-Bletchley Park members my book Secret Postings was launched in a marquee in the Bletchley Park grounds. Ann and George Keller from the USA bought a copy and came over again in 2012 to buy another. Since then we have had much email contact during which I was invited to submit my wartime story in Cryptolog, the magazine for the U.S. Naval Cryptologic Veterans Association. I did and to my amazement it appears in the Summer 2013 edition. They also published an article I wrote about my wartime billets in the Winter 2014 edition and an article about the Home Front in the Fall 2014 edition.

Crypologia has also published a lovely review of my book in an edition of the magazine (Volume 37, Number 1 2013).

Ann Keller, Charlotte Webb, Fred Hampe & George Keller, 2013
© Bletchley Park Research

For Remembrance Sunday 2013 – The Andrew Marr Show

A fellow veteran, Ruth Bourne, and I were interviewed in the library at BP by Sophie Raworth, where we gave a brief account of our roles during the war. Ruth talked about her time as a Bombe operator working at Eastcote, one of Bletchley Park's outstations during the war and I talked about my life at Bletchley Park.

HRH The Duchess of Cambridge

On Wednesday 18 June 2014 HRH the Duchess of Cambridge attended Bletchley Park to mark the completion of project Neptune, the first phase of the Heritage Lottery funded restoration of Bletchley Park.

Bletchley Park was closed to the public for this event but

there were around 500 people representing the firms who had been involved with restoration, i.e., architects, builders, engineers, and anyone connected with the rebuild as well as Trustees, a representative from McAfee, two government representatives for Poland and other people.

On arrival the guests were met by the CEO, Iain Standen, and taken into the new visitor centre in Block C. After a pleasant time talking to other guests and enjoying light refreshments the guests who were chosen to meet the Duchess of Cambridge went to the drawing room in the Mansion for a private reception. After lunch the Duchess visited every table and took the time to speak to everyone. I was presented to the Duchess by a Bletchley Park Trustee, Eileen Scanlon. The Duchess asked me about my role at Bletchley Park during the war and I told her about my transcribing work in the Japanese Section.

I am happy to say she was genuinely interested in the guests and the history of Bletchley Park.

It transpires that her maternal Grandmother, with her twin sister was employed at Bletchley Park during the war. It's nice to think that after speaking to us, the Duchess had a clearer picture of the life and work undertaken by her relatives.

After the presentations we all moved out into glorious sunshine on the lawn to hear the speeches by the Chairman of the Bletchley Park Trust, Sir John Scarlett and Mr Paul Hudson of the Heritage Lottery fund.

The park looked very festive with the long row of flags representing the nations of some of the guests, including Poland, who played such a significant part in early breaking of the Enigma machine.

After the speeches the Duchess was invited to plant a tree to commemorate the event in the lawned area by the lake. Following which the Duchess departed and the remaining guest continued to meet old friends and make new ones.

In all, a very memorable day, which I am very proud to have been involved in.

Cyber Security

Whether I talk to school children, or adults who can spread the word to their children or grandchildren I always stress cyber security as a career choice, especially for girls who are under-represented in the industry.

So it was with enormous pleasure that I attended the opening of the McAfee cyber security exhibit at Bletchley Park on 30 June 2014. It was a very social event, attended by a lot of members of the press. As usual Sir John Scarlett gave an inspiring speech, focusing on the importance of Bletchley Park's history. I did my best to give a first-hand account of life at Bletchley Park during the war. I found the day an enjoyable blend of the past and future of codebreaking.

The Women of Bletchley Park Lecture

On 20 July 2014 four women from Bletchley Park's wartime world took to the stage to be interviewed in front of a packed audience at Bletchley Park. Ruth Bourne, Gwendoline Page, Jean Valentine and I were each given the opportunity to share our stories and answer the many questions asked by the audience. It seems to me that people love to hear about the day to day routine and how we juggled our working lives with our social lives. I was particularly touched by the interest shown by so many people.

Getting the Bletchley Park story more widely known

Since 1994 I have been invited by a variety of groups (U3a, Probus, Rotary, WI, Mothers' Union, schools, British Legion and private houses) to talk about Bletchley Park's role from 1939 to 1945, my part in it and its current status as a world class heritage attraction.

I have also given telephone interviews to CNN, Ann Fisher's 'All Sides' radio show on WOSU - a local radio programme in Colombus, Ohio, USA with author Sinclair McKay and a radio programme in Birmingham.

Writing articles for the American Cryptolog magazine published by the U.S. Naval Cryptologic Veterans Association is another good way I have been able to spread the word about Bletchley Park. All of the foregoing has, I hope, given a few thousand people an insight into an amazing historic site and maybe encouraged some to read the many books on the subject written by eminent authors.

All these new adventures show that life can be really interesting, even at 91.

EPILOGUE

A Great Honour

On 9 October 2009, a little over fifty nine years since my October return to England from Washington, I was honoured to attend Bletchley Park as one of the thirty five veterans invited to attend the ceremony to celebrate the new Commemorative Badge awarded to all the surviving Bletchley Park veterans. Presented by the then Foreign Secretary, The Right Honourable David Milliband, it was truly a day to remember and it filled me with pride to know that I had served my country in a way that is honoured and remembered today and will continue to inspire future generations.

Charlotte Webb receiving the Commemorative Badge at Bletchley Park in 2009. Crown Copyright – used with the kind permission of the Director, GCHQ ©2010

APPENDICES

I have shared many photographs in the pages of this book but there are some documents extracts, particularly relating to my service in the ATS and time at The Pentagon that readers may find interesting.

APPENDIX 1   My father's report on the abandoned British Legion Police Force mission to Czechoslovakia, 1938.

APPENDIX 2   ATS Soldier's Service and Pay Book extract

APPENDIX 3   ATS and VAD Release Book extract

APPENDIX 4   Certificate of Unemployment

APPENDIX 5   Wartime Post Office Savings Deposit Form

APPENDIX 6   Wartime Brochure about The Pentagon purchased at The Pentagon in 1945

APPENDIX 7   Table of ATS personnel at Bletchley Park

APPENDIX ONE

Below is my father's report on the abandoned British Legion Police Force mission to Czechoslovakia (see Chapter 3).

BRITISH LEGION AGM
LUDLOW
21 October 1938

As a very ordinary member of the British Legion, it is a great honour to have to give an account of the all too brief life of the Volunteer Police Force, which was created almost at a moment's notice for service in Czechoslovakia. It may be called an offspring of the Legion and though it died so young, it was indeed a very sturdy child – as the events from October 5th to 15th go to prove.

To go back a few weeks to about the middle of September – the F.O. asked our National Chairman if he could raise a force of 10, 000 legionnaires should they be required.

You have no doubt about his reply.

Later, political circumstances changed the whole situation and Sir Francis Fetherston-Godley was asked again by the F.O. if he could create a body of 1200 Volunteer Police from the Legion for service at once in the Plebiscite area.

On Wednesday Oct 5th all branches received memos calling for volunteers. As time was pressing, the onus was put on the County Secretaries, who were to have the application forms before 6 o/c that evening.

The result was that in two days, 17, 000 applications had been received and the Force of 1200 complete and equipped was ready to sail on Friday night. Three days after the memos were sent out from H.Q.

On arrival at Olympia, each man received his identity card and then filed into his contingency site, one of the two galleries round the Empire Hall. After being well satisfied by Messrs J. Lyons & Co, each man filled a canvas Palliasse and pillow with straw and drew 2 blankets (or more). After which it was not long before every man had received his blue suit and badge, belt, stick, gloves and Legion tie, haversack, water bottle, 2 shirts, 2 towels and cleaning materials. Metropolitan police great coats and caps, the next morning, completed the issue.

The Force had its own fleet of Bedford Motor Vans and motorcycles for despatch riders and a St Johns Ambulance unit.

On the Saturday morning, the whole Force marched out with the Band of the Welsh Guards. The Legion standard bearer alongside the Guards Colours made a fine show. The O.C. addressed the Force in Empire Hall after the parade and expressed his appreciation of the performance. Twenty years after demobilization (from the First World War 1918) and every man marching with a swing. He added the main point of the march was to see if the boots pinched!

Sir Philip Morris also gave the Force a cheery address and told how he had flown over to see Herr Hitler who cordially welcomed the scheme and said when the BLVPF was used in the Plebiscite areas, German troops would not be employed. On this occasion too, General Sir Ian Hamilton mounted a trestle table and gave his welcome and was greeted with the most tremendous cheers.

Lady Spencer Churchill, who had taken charge of the comforts of the men, had a great reception when she announced that she had rung up Imperial Tobacco Co and asked for 60, 000 cigarettes "on tick". The reply was "no tick, you can have them".

Following a senior officer's visit to the Foreign Office the Plebescite would not take place and the consequently the operation was cancelled.

I have been unable to find out any further information about the exercise, but I hope that someone reading this may be able to add more information.

APPENDIX TWO

ATS PAY BOOK

Army Book 64 (Part I)

Soldier's Service Book.

(Soldier's Pay Book, Army Book 64 (Part II), will be
issued for active service.)

Entries in this book (other than those connected with the
making of a Soldier's Will and insertion of the names of
relatives) are to be made under the superintendence of an
Officer.

Instructions to Soldier.

1. You are held **personally responsible** for the safe
custody of this book.

2. You will **always carry this book** on your person.

3. You must produce the book whenever called upon
to do so by a competent military authority, viz., Officer, Warrant Officer, N.C.O. or Military Policeman.

4. You must not alter or make any entry in this book
(except as regards your next-of-kin on pages 10 and 11 or
your Will on pages 15 to 20).

5. Should you lose the book, you will report the matter
to your immediate military superior.

6. On your transfer to the Army Reserve this book will be
handed into your Orderly Room for transmission, through the
O. i/c Records, to place of rejoining on mobilization.

7. You will be permitted to retain this book after
discharge, but should you lose the book after discharge it
cannot be replaced.

8. If you are discharged from the Army Reserve, this book
will be forwarded to you by the O. i/c Records.

2

(I) SOLDIER'S NAME and DESCRIPTION on ATTESTATION.

Army Number ...W/82948

Surname (in capitals) VINE-STEVENS

Christian Names (in full) Charlotte Elizabeth

Date of Birth....13:5:23

Place of Birth.
- Parish ....
- In or near the town of ████████
- In the county of ████████

Trade on Enlistment... Student of Music, Language + Domestic Science

Nationality of Father at birth ████

Nationality of Mother at birth ████

Religious Denomination ...C of E..

Approved Society ..~~Shrewsbury~~..

Membership No. ....

Enlisted at Shrewsbury On 3rd Sept. 41.

For the :—
- ~~* Regular Army.~~ A. T. S. ~~* Supplementary Reserve.~~
- ~~* Territorial Army.~~ ~~* Army Reserve Section D.~~

Duration * Strike out those inapplicable.

For............years with the Colours and............years in the Reserve.

Signature of Soldier C. E. Vine Stevens

Date.......12/9/41

3

DESCRIPTION ON ENLISTMENT.

Height ...5...ft. ...4.2.ins.   Weight ...153...lbs.

Maximum Chest ....ins.   Complexion...............

Eyes ..Blue grey...........   Hair .Mid Brown.

Distinctive Marks and Minor Defects ....

....

....

....

....

....

....

....

CONDITION ON TRANSFER TO RESERVE.

Found fit for ....

Defects or History of past illness which should be

enquired into if called up for Service ....

....

....

....

....

....

Date.................19.........

Initials of M.O. i/c...

▲ 2

APPENDICES

4

PARTICULARS OF TRAINING.

Courses and Schools. Specialist Qualifications. Showing result.	Date.	Initials of Officer.
Appd A/P/Cpl w/ef.	18.5.42	
Pt II order 30/43		
Conf WS Cpl w/ef.	14.8.43	
Pt II order 60/43		
issued 2 t/bar service chevs	9.5.44	
P/A/Sgt.	21.8.44	
WS /Sgt	17.2.45	
Promoted A/R/S/59/	15.3.45	
w/ef 1/1/3/9/	15.7.45	

RECORD OF EMPLOYMENT AS AN ARMY TRADESMAN.
(For men in receipt of tradesmen's rates of pay only.)

Trade.	Group.	Class.	Remarks, e.g., On enlistment; Re-classified; Re-mustered, etc.	Date.	Initials of Officer.
Clerk	—	11	Mustered filling 28.10.41		
			Vacancy ab ovab in RAOC Pt.II No.41.S		
			Pt.II No 26		
			dated 26.12.41		
Clerk		1	Passed trade test 1.6.42		
			certified qualified Pt.II No 42 x/6.6.42		

RECORD OF SPECIALIST EMPLOYMENT WHILST SERVING.*

Period.		Nature of Employment.	Remarks and Initials of Officer.
From	To		
29.12.41.		Appt'd P/A/L/Cpl. w.e.f. 5.11.41. Pt. II No. 25 dated	
20.8.43		20.11.41. Confd. A/u/L/Cpl. w.e.f. 15/8/43 Pt. II No. 27 dated 20-8-43	
10.10.41		Granted W.S. Rank Cpl. w.e.f. 16 Aug 43.	
18.3.42		14 day Dleave	
		C.N.O. RATION CARDS	
		Issued new Card P.B. Period 1.3.42.-31.6.43	

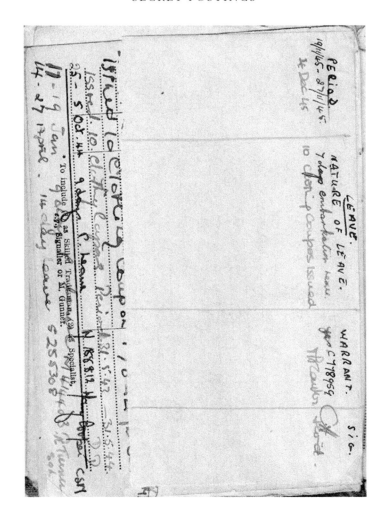

APPENDIX THREE

ATS RELEASE BOOK

ARMY BOOK X 802

Surname _Vine-Stevens_

Initials _C.E._

Army No. _W/82948_

A.T.S. AND V.A.D.
RELEASE BOOK

CLASS "A"

Any person finding this Book is requested to hand it in to any Barracks, Post Office, or Police Station, for transmission to the Under Secretary of State, The War Office, London, S.W.I.

This book must be presented at the Post Office whenever you cash a postal draft or one of the drafts in your payment book, to enable the Post Office Official to record the date of payment on the inside page of the front cover.

51-9848

PART I

INSTRUCTIONS TO RELEASED PERSON

MEDICAL TREATMENT AFTER LEAVING MILITARY DISPERSAL UNIT

You are now entitled to medical benefit under the National Health Insurance Acts, and a medical card telling you how to get treatment will be sent to you as soon as possible.

Medical benefit includes free treatment from an insurance doctor at his surgery (or if your condition requires it, at your home), and free medicine.

If you go back to live in your old district and had an insurance doctor before you joined up you will be restored to his list if he is still in practice himself or by deputy.

If you fall ill before the medical card comes, fill in the application below and find this book to your previous insurance doctor (or, if absent, his deputy). If you did not have an insurance doctor before you joined up or if you go to live in another part of the country, apply to any insurance doctor. You can see a list of insurance doctors at the local Post Office.

Do not detach this form from the book. The doctor will do this.

PART II.—To be completed in Unit

Rank ...W/S...S|S|v....................... Number ...W|.87248............

Initials ...S.E.................... Surname (Block Letters) ...V.N.E...STEVENS.

Date of Birth. 13. 5. 23........ Sex ....F........ (If a married woman, state maiden name)

The above-named individual left this Military Dispersal Unit on the date shown in the stamp opposite.

Form Med. 50A
Military Dispersal
Unit Stamp

PART II

Available for three months from date of leaving Military Dispersal Unit.

To be completed by released person ONLY if no medical treatment is before a medical card is received.

I have NOT received a medical card since leaving the Military Dispersal Unit and hereby apply for a medical card to be issued to me.

Delete as { I was on the list of Dr. ....before I was mobilised or called up for service.
may be { I was not on the list of a doctor in the district where I am now, and desire to be placed on the list of ....
necessary (Insert name of doctor or approved institution.)

My present address is ....

Do you intend to leave this district within three months from the date hereof? If so when ?.................

Name of Approved Society* (if any)...
  (If a deposit contributor write ". D.C.")
Name of Branch (if any) of Society ....
Membership number.......................

Date ....

(Signature of released individual.)

* If you were a member of an Approved Society before you were mobilised or called up for service, or if you joined an Approved Society during service, your membership is still effective.

(See also overleaf.)

APPENDIX FOUR

CERTIFICATE OF UNEMPLOYMENT

87177   Army Form X202/D (Revised).

CERTIFICATE OF RELEGATION TO THE UNEMPLOYED LIST OF A.T.S. AUXILIARY OR V.A.D. MEMBER

Army No. *W/82948*   Rank *P/A/S/Sgt*

Surname (Block letters) *VINE-STEVENS*

Christian Name/s *Charlotte Elizabeth*

Corps *A.T.S*

The relegation to the Unemployed List of the above-named is confirmed with effect from* *14-4-46*

Record Office Stamp.

A.T.S. RECORD OFFICE
7 MAR 1946
WINCHESTER

Date ....

Officer i/c *A.T.S* Records.

* The date to be inserted here will be that following the day on which Release Leave terminates, including any additional leave to which the Auxiliary or V.A.D. Member may be entitled by virtue of service overseas.

Wt. 24239/6707   200M   9/45   KJL/971/16   Gp. 38/3

APPENDIX FIVE

WARTIME POST OFFICE SAVINGS DEPOSIT FORM

To .... W/82948 S/Sgt. Vine - Stevens b.g.   **PAY FORM R.16**

RELEASE.   **97450**

POST OFFICE SAVINGS BANK ACCOUNT No. .... *

I   The amount of War Gratuity and Post War Credit as shown below is being deposited in your name in the Post Office Savings Bank :—

		£	s.	d.
WAR GRATUITY	51 months at 10/8 per month	27	4	1
(Note—The period of Release and Overseas leave does NOT count as service for the assessment of War Gratuity)	Less deductions (brief particulars)			
	Balance of War Gratuity due	27	4	—
POST WAR CREDITS DUE From 1/1/42 to 13/4/46		25	3	4
OTHER CREDITS				
TOTAL AMOUNT DEPOSITED IN POST OFFICE SAVINGS BANK		£ 52	7	4

84584

P.T.O.

2 The deposit will be made on the fifty-seventh day following the date you left the Military Dispersal Unit.

3 A Post Office Savings Bank Book will be sent to you in due course by the Director, Post Office Savings Department.

4 If you change your address after receiving this form, you should at once send a postcard to :—

THE DIRECTOR,

POST OFFICE SAVINGS DEPARTMENT,

25 CHURCH STREET,

MANCHESTER, 4.

The postcard should be prepared as follows :—

---

(1) ARMY NUMBER   (2) RANK AND NAME, IN BLOCK CAPITALS

(3) REGIMENT OR CORPS (4) RELEASE POST OFFICE SAVINGS BANK ACCOUNT NUMBER (see * at top of this form, overleaf).

Please note change of address to which all communications should be sent.
   (New Address in full)   (Date)   (Signature)

Paymaster's
Authenticating
Stamp :—

(1676) 55364 3960B/D.5314 1,000,000 1/46 SP/TBH **Gp. 38**

J.10067

APPENDIX SIX

Building The Pentagon 1941 - 1943

The Pentagon designed in a race against time and was planned for efficiency, not beauty.

The design of concentric pentagons wasn't seriously considered until 8 August 1941 and the subsequent preliminary design and drafting work took thirty four days.

Construction started on 11 September 1941 and completed on 15 January 1943. At one stage 15,000 men were employed to build it. A staggering 32,000 worked within its walls daily and for a few months during 1945, I was one of them.

Visitor are required to report to Reception. The receptionists are 'chosen for their neatness, attractive appearance, tact, quick wit, and general good sense.'

Ramps lead from the Concourse to the various floors.

Guards posted at the doorways to the ramps check military passes and civilians' badges. Bags, packages and papers are thoroughly inspected.

A plan of the building is posted on each floor. This copy gives an example of room 4D-620. It is on the 4th floor (indicated by 4) and located in the 4th ring (D). The 3rd number (6) indicates the corridor and the last 2 digits are the room's location in the corridor. Each floor has an identical layout so they are decorated in different colours to help orientate the employees.

Staff work in open plan offices

Mail and official documents are delivered by messengers on tricycles as well as by pneumatic tubes, which shoot documents to one of the five tube stations on each floor.

Huge quantities of foodstuffs are consumed daily: 5,055 pounds of meat, fish, and poultry; 15,361 pounds of milk and milk products; 4,153 pounds of potatoes; 4,387 pounds of leafy green and yellow vegetables. Pentagonians eat every day 826 loaves of bread, 1,183 dozen rolls and muffins, 7,003 pieces of pie, 418 gallons of ice cream, 728 dozen eggs, 382 heads of lettuce, 225 pounds of bacon, and 82 gallons of gravy.

Waiting for the bus at The Pentagon

Christmas Service held in the central courtyard at The Pentagon.

APPENDIX SEVEN

TABLE OF ATS PERSONNEL & TOTAL NUMBER OF WOMEN IN ALL SERVICES AT BLETCHLEY PARK

1942		Women (ATS)			Total Women in all Services		
		Officers	Other Ranks	Total	Officers	Other Ranks	Total
March	22			37			358
	29			38			362
April	5			37			362
	12			37			369
	19			38			381
	26			38			387
May	3			39			398
	10			77			454
	17			77			474
	24			79			491
	31			79			506
June	7			82			513
	14			82			528
	21			82			548
	28			85			566
July	5			85			580
	12			86			592
	19			86			608
	26			99			639

1942		Women (ATS)			Total Women in all Services		
		Officers	Other Ranks	Total	Officers	Other Ranks	Total
August	2			101			661
	9			105			673
	16			105			679
	23			106			738
	30			122			783
September	6			126			814
	13			121			842
	20			120			853
	27			120			880
October	4			120			893
	11			127			925
	18			141			956
	25			144			968
November	1			147			963
	8			148			967
	15			150			966
	22			155			977
	29			154			979
December	6			162			985
	13			162			982
	20			162			993
	27			164			1000

1943		Women (ATS)			Total Women in all Services		
		Officers	Other Ranks	Total	Officers	Other Ranks	Total
January	3			152			995
	10			168			1010
	17			187			1028
	24			186			1030
	31			186			1029
February	7			185			1030
	14			185			1018
	21			184			1014
	28			196			1039
March	7			197			1324
	14			197			1344
	21			197			1392
	28			201			1411
April	4			203			1428
	11			204			1446
	18			207			1474
	25			207			1479
May	2			216			1520
	9			220			1547
	16			227			1575
	23			226			1597
	30			227			1683
June	6			228			1704
	13			252			1741
	20			258			1765
	27			259			1770

1943		Women (ATS)			Total Women in all Services		
		Officers	Other Ranks	Total	Officers	Other Ranks	Total
July	4			261			1783
	11			260			1789
	18			262			1808
	25			262			1807
August	1			267			1829
	8			271			1829
	15			270			1837
	22			271			1847
	29			271			1863
September	5			273			1863
	12			283			1881
	19			281			1946
	26			285			1957
October	3			289			1983
	10			287			2001
	17			292			2016
	24			292			2038
	31			301			2085
November	7			302			2123
	14			305			2224
	21			306			2345
	28			313			2477
December	5			316			2570
	12			324			2639
	19			336			2729
	26			335			2887

1944		Women (ATS)			Total Women in all Services		
		Officers	Other Ranks	Total	Officers	Other Ranks	Total
January	2			335			2871
	9			340			2849
	16			362			2944
	23			363			2943
	30			363			2985
February	6			363			2996
	13			364			2989
	20			364			2999
	27			364			2998
March	5			365			3005
	12			378			3044
	19			378			3055
	26			378			3086
April	2			390			3132
	9			400			3138
	16			400			3177
	23			399			3151
	30			402			3096
May	7			402			3111
	14			400			3203
	21			399			3184
	28			397			3144
June	4			398			3161
	11			398			3236
	18			399			3251
	25			399			3311

1944		Women (ATS)			Total Women in all Services		
		Officers	Other Ranks	Total	Officers	Other Ranks	Total
July	2			399			3357
	9			399			3410
	16			400			3440
	23			403			3490
	30			403			3509
August	6			402			3549
	13			411			3569
	20			412			3582
	27			408			3622
September	3			402			3671
	10			400			3727
	17			397			3755
	24			395			3786
October	1			395			3802
	8	70	331	401	183	3676	3859
	15	70	331	401	182	3732	3914
	22	73	330	403	187	3755	3942
	29	73	330	403	188	3767	3955
November	5	73	336	409	188	3771	3959
	12	73	337	410	189	3786	3975
	19	73	337	410	193	3795	3988
	26	74	338	412	194	3805	3999
December	3	74	338	412	193	3819	4012
	10	81	332	413	203	3832	4035
	17	81	331	412	203	3853	4056
	24	74	338	412	197	3864	4061
	31	77	334	411	199	3887	4086

1945		Women (ATS)			Total Women in all Services		
		Officers	Other Ranks	Total	Officers	Other Ranks	Total
January	7	77	333	410	198	3888	4086
	14	77	331	408	199	3900	4099
	21	77	332	409	199	3896	4095
	28	77	337	414	208	3901	4109
February	4	73	335	408	206	3898	4104
	11	73	332	405	206	3883	4089
	18	73	332	405	205	3878	4083
	25	73	330	403	205	3855	4060
March	4	74	328	402	201	3899	4100
	11	73	328	401	196	3914	4110
	18	73	326	399	196	3926	4122
	25	73	326	399	195	3934	4129
April	1	73	322	395	193	3928	4121
	8	73	321	394	194	3916	4110
	15	73	330	403	194	3928	4122
	22	71	333	404	192	3926	4118
	29	69	334	403	189	3948	4137
May	6	69	334	403	190	3957	4147
	13	69	336	405	189	3951	4140
	20	69	336	405	180	3954	4134
	27	69	333	402	176	3911	4087
June	3	67	336	403	175	3869	4044
	10	67	336	403	166	3804	3970
	17	66	335	401	162	3657	3819
	24	65	335	400	157	2814	2971

1945		Women (ATS)			Total Women in all Service		
		Officers	Other Ranks	Total	Officers	Other Ranks	Total
July	1	61	331	392	153	3249	3402
	8	60	325	385	150	3121	3271
	15	57	317	374	145	2901	3046
	22	58	295	353	141	2830	2971
	29	58	293	351	142	2661	2803
August	5	55	289	344	138	2555	2693
	12	54	272	326	135	2270	2405
	19	52	267	319	131	2213	2344
	26	51	265	316	125	2003	2128

These tables are reproduced from 'Figuring It Out at Bletchley Park' with permission of the authors, Kerry Howard and John Gallehawk.

GLOSSARY

ATS	Auxiliary Territorial Service – the women's Army.
Block F	One of largest blocks, which was first occupied in November 1943.
FO	Foreign Office
GC&CS	Government Code and Cypher School
Hut 4	Codebreaking hut built in 1939 to house the Naval Section until it moved to Block A in 1942. The Military Section took over the hut but not the name.
NAAFI	Navy, Army, Air Force Institutes providing catering facilities such as canteens, shops etc.
NIRD	National Institute of Research Diaries
PNEU	Parents National Educational Union
PSO	Permanent Staff Officer
QARANC	Queen Alexandra's Royal Army Nursing Corps
RAF	Royal Air Force
RCAF	Royal Canadian Air Force
TA	Territorial Army
WAAF	Women's Auxiliary Air Force
WRAC	Women's Royal Army Corps (replaced the ATS on 1 February 1949)
WRNS	Women's Royal Naval Service, often referred to as WRENS
YWCA	Young Women's Christian Association

INDEX

FIND OUT MORE

Thank you for taking the time to read my book. I hope you have enjoyed it. If you did I would be grateful if you could post a short review on Amazon, GoodReads or your preferred book seller's website. You can also help me spread the word by sharing details of the book on social media.

You can find the links to some of the articles and programmes mentioned in Chapter Nine by visiting:

www.bletchleyparkresearch.co.uk/authors-researchers/charlotte-webb

News of future events I attend will also appear on Kerry Howard's Bletchley Park Research website. **Sign up for the newsletter** at to keep up to date on my adventures as well as other Bletchley Park related news.

www.bletchleyparkresearch.co.uk

This book has been produced by Charlotte Webb in partnership with BookTower Publishing. You can find out more about their other Bletchley Park and World War 2 codebreaking books by visiting:

www.booktowerpublishing.co.uk.

You can find out more about the work of the Bletchley Park Trust - the official 'Home of the Codebreakers' at:

www.bletchleypark.org.uk

ALL RANKS.

" REMEMBER—Never discuss military, naval or air matters in public or with any stranger, no matter to what nationality he or she may belong.

The enemy wants information about you, your unit, your destination. He will do his utmost to discover it.

Keep him in the dark. Gossip on military subjects is highly dangerous to the country, whereas secrecy leads to success.

BE ON YOUR GUARD and report any suspicious individual."

Printed in Great Britain
by Amazon

63764856R00078